Best love Mahon

The Moon's Daughter

Marion Moynihan

The Moon's Daughter
is published by
DOGHOUSE
P.O. Box 312
Tralee G.P.O.
Co. Kerry
Ireland

€12.00

167,432

TEL: +353 (0)66 7137547
www.doghousebooks.ie   email: doghouse312@eircom.net

Copyright : Marion Moynihan, June, 2006

ISBN 0-9552003-1-8 / 978-0-9552003-1-1

The author and publisher thanks Galway County Council
for the 2006 Publication Assistance Award.

Thanks to Cumas Teo, Connemara for their financial support.

GALWAY COUNTY LIBRARIES

For sponsoring the launches of this book we thank
Moynihan & Moynihan Chemicals, Douglas, Cork
Ivan O'Sullivan, Roofing Contractor, Kanturk, Co Cork
The Four Faced Liar Bar, Manhattan, New York

Edited for DOGHOUSE by Noel King

Cover image: "Self Portrait", Marion Moynihan

Printed by Tralee Printing Works, Denny Street, Tralee

Further copies available at €12, post free, from the above address, cheques etc.
payable to DOGHOUSE also PAYPAL - www.paypal.com or
doghousepaypal@eircom.net

Doghouse is a non-profit taking company, aiming to publish the best of
literary works by Irish born writers. Donations are welcome and will be
acknowledged on this page.

for my late mother and father,
Dan and Kitty Moynihan

Acknowledgments are due to the editors of the following in which many of these poems, or versions of them, were first published:

A Sense of Cork 1999 (Ed. Patrick Galvin & Patricia Casey); Asylum Arts Journal; Cork Literary Review (Ed. Eugene O'Connell); Cork Literary Review (Ed. Catherine-Ann O'Connell); Turbulence: Corrib Voices (Ed. Helena Mulkerns; Crannóg (Ed. Ciaran Parks); Cúm (Ed. Moya Cannon); Divas 11(Ed. Nuala Ní Concubhair); The Edgeworth Papers; The Enchanted Way (RTE Radio One); Heart of Kerry (Ed. Noel King); Podium 11, Podium 111, Podium 1V; Podium V (Ed. Noel King); Ropes –The Review of Post Graduate Studies NUIG; The Sunday Tribune; Women's Work V11; Words (Ed. Marion Moynihan).

Thanks to:

Neil Bedford, Neil and Carmel Moynihan, my sons Conor, Ivan and Ronan and their wives, and all my girlfriends for their love and support always.

Rita Ann Higgins, Aidan Hayes, Michael Gorman, and Vincent Woods.

Louis de Paor, and Galway City Library, to Joanne Keane O'Flynn and Kanturk Branch Library for the launches of this book.

The members of the Tralee Scribblers and Fia Rua (Killarney) Writers' Groups for invaluable support, comradeship and critique;

Mary Immaculate College, Limerick; NUIG, Galway and Thomas Moore College, Kentucky, USA.

Noel King, Editor, DOGHOUSE books.

What would happen if one woman told the truth about her life?
The world would split open

from the poem *Käthe Kollwitz* **by Muriel Rukeyser**

Contents

The Moon's Daughter

I am the moon's daughter –
I ebb and flow and drown in cycles.

Last night
I talked to my moon-sister,
told her I hated her,
her bitchiness,
how nothing is ever right,
how she evens scores,
takes revenge.
She bears no resemblance to me
though we have the same father
and the same mother.
My mother noticed when I was thirteen
said I was a lovely child... till then.

Oh Goddess of the moon
tonight take a piece of paper
in my planetary colour,
light it with a candle
and wait till it burns down.
Persephone, Levanah, Aphrodite,
guide me towards the phase
of sagging breasts and dry vaginas.

I never asked to be young.

Fairyhill

Long hot summers spent at my grandmother's –
rumours of spells, dells of purple foxglove,
fairy forts left untouched on neighbour's land;
squatting in the acre, dock leaves to wipe your bottom,
groundsel to feed the hens.

Dressing up in her black shawl, playing at being old,
walking the roads, waiting for Moll to come from the Hosiery,
my grandmother laughing, buttering warm crusty bread.

Sunday mornings, driving to mass in the pony and trap,
rugs hugging our knees, midges singing in our hair,
pocket-money for a week's supply of gallon sweets,
a glass of lemonade in the dark and dingy pub.

Days filled easily between collecting the milk from Walsh's yard
and climbing down the stone steps to the spring well.

Corpus Christi

Forty years ago
an old man refused me flowers.
I had the white dress,
the veil, the silver basket.
He had a small galvanized house,
a half-door and dozens of dahlias.

Every time I passed
I looked, I plucked, I peeled,
with eyes as big and watery
as the insides of cucumbers.

Nearer my God to Thee
reverberated from telegraph poles,
the monosyllabic sound
of the rosary never far away.

His house is gone now,
there are no signs of dahlias.
Last night I dreamt
that dahlias grew in hell,
but it's forty years too late.

The Barber

Every day I brought your dinner in a raffia message bag
on a saucepan of boiling water to keep it warm.
Every day you gave me a thrupenny bit.

I'd climb that narrow twisted stairs to reach
the glass door with the adverts for Gillette blades,
Palmolive soap and tinned toothpaste.

Through the gaps in the ads I could count
the heads the full width of the gilt mirror.
The room hummed with cigarette smoke and Bay Rum

as you collected clumps of hair in a tortoiseshell comb.
You would reach deep into the wooden drawer
for the thrupenny bit, your fingers stained from nicotine.

You were supposed to look like Victor Mature,
that same cowboy stance, lips full and pouting,
the faraway look of the Sunday matinee idol.

You could talk on any subject: hurling, football, politics,
careful never to show your true colours,
you only discussed religion when drunk.

My mother scoured combs, washed towels, brushed clippings,
counted the money and ran the tinkers from the door.
I learnt about the fuss to find a freshly laundered gown

for the Canon, shook out on your knees with the crack
of a circus whip, and I noticed your voice would change.
The men in the queue stayed silent and read comics;

we could only whisper in the makeshift kitchen.
During quiet times you fixed electric razors
and old watches – an eyeglass stuck in your socket –

or carved little wooden figures,
shaving them into a black cast-iron fireplace.
You made us a rocking-duck for Christmas,

stayed up all night to finish the Delph dresser.
My mother burnt the duck for firewood like she dumped
your rosebush because it had thorns.

Then you began slipping into Jamsie Johns for the poker,
the whist, the pool, the darts; began missing the Sunday dinner.
When I pleaded with you to come home I'd get another thrupenny bit.

I remember the shouting when you should have been silent,
the silence the many times you should have shouted
and my mother's laugh becoming shallower by the day.

The Breadmakers

I resist the temptation to press down hard
to cut deep into the dough the sign of the cross,
while images ooze of summers in Fairyhill,
of an old woman held together
by a wrap-around apron,
lifting her cake of white bread
flat and oval like a beach
from the bastable,
the smell reaching as far
as the apple blossom in the acre.
She places it upright on a table
under which stand white enamel buckets
of clear spring water.
At supper she saws long thin slices
towards her chest,
the heel firmly tucked into her side
as if she were playing a violin.
She would wipe wisps of white hair
springing from a bun at the back of her head
and sometimes exasperated
she would release the bun into her hand,
wind it back again around her finger
holding it together with just one long hairpin.
Her puckered lined mouth said it all –
this woman had no time for shop bread.

Mother Tongue

She was a dab hand at killing fleas
and would squeeze them between
her thumbnails until she heard them
crack and had drawn blood; the buggers
like a smear on a microscope slide.
We picked them up in the Cosey Cinema,
nick-named the *Flea Pit*, or off the greyhounds
before they were doused with the DDT.
She was a dinger at killing rabbits too,
tying a string to their back legs;
teasing the greyhound smart enough
to suss out the stuffed hare at the track.
She was good at killing things alright –
her tongue being her first weapon of choice.

The Wheelwright

My mother mentioned words like felloes, dowels, axles and half-axles,
told us about apprentices she fed, who had been nicked in the ear
for using spoke-shave instead of the more delicate sandpaper.

   Her father could distinguish the heart of the oak from the sap,
   carry the spokes to his bench and plane them through and through.
   With compasses and bevel he marked out the shoulders.

She told us stories at night about the hospital in Millstreet,
the Diphtheria, about missing her First Holy Communion,
about not being told why her mother never came home.

   Her father cut out the foot with a fine tenon saw –
   the tenon to be driven down into the nave –
   all the time shaping the parts of the spoke to be exposed.

She ran away at nineteen to marry my father,
a waster, she was told, an Artisan on the Marriage Cert.
It was fifteen years before she and her father spoke.

   Her father used an axe and a drawshave – chopping out the face,
   splintering away the four corners – before a smoothing-plane
   made the sides of the spokes straight.

I spent my childhood in that workshop with those bright orange carts
not recognising the symmetry of the sides, but mesmerised all the same
by the rhythm of my grandfather planing wood and whistling –

waiting patiently for the shavings to drop like ringlets to the floor.

Annie Larkin

Annie Larkin was not like the rest of us,
seven feet tall and that *here's my head*
my arse is coming syndrome.
She had an articulated jaw
but no visible teeth
and relished an audience
with thirty young girls.

Her visit was timed
to coincide with our sewing class
where we hem-stitched
and slip-stitched
to Annie's tall tales
of gossip and carrying-on,
her lanky body spilling over
onto Sr Augustine's desk
where she was warm
and dry for an hour at least.

One Saturday night in Babe's corner shop
she gave me the price of my first dance,
an open air ceilí in Bill Sullivan's yard
a mile outside the town,
a godsend with parents gone to the dogs
– they often went to the dogs.

I will never forget it for her
or the taste of fried eggs from Tweetie,
the boy who brought me home, gave me my first kiss.
For years afterwards I would pass the bothán
that was her home covered over with briars and wild roses,
seeing her stoop again as she entered the door
wondering if her head touched the ceiling,
convinced that she gave me her last sixpence.

Cat And Mouse

I can identify with the mouse
I know what it's like to be swallowed whole.

Maybe swallowed whole is too strong
I saw him eat the head first.
He left the gallbladder,
the bile, the bitter taste.

He is a house cat
he sleeps on my bed every night.

The Sixties

I missed the revolution,
for me the sex wasn't free,
every month I paid in confession,
every month I got ten *Hail Marys*
until some guy got wise
and gave me the *Stations of the Cross*.

Then I started my own revolution,
I stopped going to mass,
I discovered orgasms,
I left my husband,
the one I dressed in white for;
the one I missed the revolution for.

When Children Stop Believing

She filled their stockings with Polish coal
because she didn't want to be fooled.

She watched their eyes fill up,
that will toughen them, she said.

One of them toughened up so much
he ended up beating his wife,

spending most of his time in the pub;
a battering ram refusing to make eye contact.

Leylandii

He clips her hedges tight
and cuts the tops off trees,
leaving them the same height,
the same distance apart.

Leylandii break the breeze
while she goes to bingo,
Kanturk, Banteer, Boherbue,
finding security in familiar faces.

She votes and goes to mass,
minds other people's children
and has no need to visit the Pyramids,
Taj Mahal or the Great Wall.

In his mind's eye with every clip
he scores a goal from centre field,
wins the Christmas Hamper at the cards,
has the fairy in the acre kneeling between his legs.

Vincent And Me

You too were mad.
You too were a failure.
You too were dependant on a brother.

Isn't it odd then,
how your sunflowers bloomed,
your cornfields ripened
and your cypresses pointed upwards.

I searched and searched for the darkness
finding it only briefly in oil-slicked crows
but even then the madness wavered
in the ambivalence of your cornfields.

But for me it was the yellow,
that sulphurous, sulphurous yellow.

Lunch At The Crawford

Amid the yackity-yak
the breastsucklers of hyperbole
wait to be seated.

A child, a taker-off of accents,
ascends and descends
tone incanting rich and poor;

the latter not here to defend themselves
for this is a conclave of the rich
and Opera House famous.

Bags drop nonchalantly
carrying the United Colours of Benetton.
Electrolysised chins wag incessantly

and waxed legs dangle delicately
willing the bottles of red wine
to body temperature.

A cold carved stone fireplace
creates a decadence and ambience
due only to popes and kings.

Food is served on plates
designed to feed the little people,
but the commoner requests more spuds

and lets the cat out of her Gucci bag.

A New Moon

in memory of Pat Browne

She cleaned the moon with a Brillo pad
and though it was a new moon
took a knife to its crustaceans.

The moon bled and wept

but there was no telling her
that some things are self-cleansing:
a woman's vagina
a man's soul
a new moon.

Hurry Up And Get Old

It's Friday and there's a smell of fish.
The pensioners gather; the men to themselves,
the women chattering, planning their next outing.
One woman asks me to have tea,
another tells me about her trips to Cork,
about the bus that leaves at ten past seven,
Who wants to be up for ten past seven?
Mrs Griffin moans about the lack of train travel
from a town that's very hard to get out of.
Sr Helen dishes out stewed apple and custard
and Mrs Daly tells me to *Hurry up and get old*!
Outside, women with funereal faces,
not old enough for free travel,
not young enough for discos,
pass their reflections in empty shop windows.
In a town that's very hard to get out of
better to *Hurry up and get old! Hurry up and get old!*

You Tell Us To *Be Something*

and I am a bell in a room
on the top floor of a big house
higher than Patrick's Hill.

Bean bags are scattered
on bare wooden floors,
the place reeks of incense.

I swirl shyly at first
slowly gathering momentum
until I am free.

I could easily be a New Year
but I am the bell ringing it in.
There are no parties,

no announcement in the paper,
no caption saying *Dead woman comes to life,
is reunited with herself.* The room swims.

The clapper stops dead at the Georgian window
level with seagulls circling the quays
level with all the church spires of Cork.

Next day as only a woman would
I bought three brass bells before leaving,
knowing that from then on I could be anything.

Pet Names

When anybody asks me
what my cat's name is
I reluctantly say *Puss.*
How original, they say,
how creative for a poet.
Of course I regret not calling him
something intellectual like Grimalkin,
though he was originally called Sooty,
he being an all-white cat.

Now, when nobody's around
I call him Pishkins, Puddingtat,
Scutterbums, and Lammy-chop-chops.
We communicate, I talk,
he moves his tail to words like
birdies, brekkies, wanna go out.
Intelligence aside,
I have buried my face
in his soft fur many times
and called him *Puss.*

Woman Talk

for Nonie

Within sight of that big bronze stag,
with the heat of the sun on her breasts
she ignores the road-rage sound of horns
before pulling onto the hard shoulder
of the new Mallow to Cork road.
Lorry drivers wonder if this woman knows
if she is coming or going.
We laugh, talk of unspeakable things
hot and clammy as the weather,
tribal as football, steamy as Playboy,
until we both notice a fly sweating on the wall.

Blennerville Bridge

I used to love the anticipation,

but most times the coast was clear —
I'd scoot across like a madwoman
with wild acceleration.

If I did meet something
I'd ease myself through
with the minimum of fuss
being able to gauge distance
like a greyhound at the first bend.

I loved the challenge of its narrowness
and the time it took
to get from one end to the other,
safely and defiantly
without indentation.

But now I want to get out
where the bridge is strongest,
tell the man in the hard hat
what I think of his alterations.

I want to ask him not to silence
the mouth of the bay with stones,
(as a means of compensation).

Being a woman of my word,
I promise I will concentrate on my driving
and only barely glance sideways at the view.

Camping In France

I am particular about the aspect –
corner site preferably,
fig tree or two for shade,
as near as possible to showers,
a safe distance from night noise,
and of course, south or south-west facing.
He gets impatient with me
a site is just a site, he says,
a place to pitch your tent.

Dressing The Bed

There's a love poem
brewing inside my head
as I listen to a bird
clear and shrill
and matter of fact
resonate your song.

You tell me
I toss your sheets
and let your
hot tap drip.

I leave myself
wide open
to criticism
during long nights of passion.

Secret Life

A man died yesterday
who still had dreams
of sailing the Caribbean.
His unfinished boat
burgeons through his garage
only yards from the sea.
His secret life in a skip
the other side of town.

Tongue Tied

If you ask me once more
if I'd like a cup of tea
I'll scream.

I'll scream so loud
that my tonsils
or what remains of them

will stick to a tree
at the other side of the road
and my tongue

will sit nicely
at the edge of Fenit pier
floodlit by night

and the sound of my scream
will hollow a hole
in the ocean bed

big enough for the two of us
and maybe then you'll know
it's not tea I'm after.

Trees

This is not a therapy poem
this is a poem about trees,
trees that sap the sun
drain the earth.
But trees don't feel
or fall out of love.
Trees don't need valium
to calm their branches
on wild and windy days.
Trees can drink a lot
and never become alcoholic.
Have you ever seen a tree cry?
I've tried to hug trees
but they never respond;
a leaf might shiver,
a branch might spring
but they never hug you back.
They can be wind stripped
and never show their angry side.
What would the roar of a tree sound like?
Would it drown out the rustle of its leaves,
a tree in pain, hurt that someone
would want to cut it down,
break its spirit for no reason?
Would it turn its anger inwards?
Where would it show?
Maybe that's why some autumn leaves
refuse to scrunch.

Egos Disturb Me

I remember a night
close to the equinox
searching for a house outside Dingle,
blue dolphins on the gable wall,
candles and joss sticks burning inside
and an all-American accent
telling me to leave my shoes
and my ego outside the door.

Since then egos disturb me,
I can walk into a room and feel one,
I can see the shape it takes and why it evolved,
the craving for centre stage,
the need to be noticed,
the way it deflects auras,
shatters chakras,
puts people on the defensive.

Now I know why
the child who was never good enough
can only leave her shoes outside the door.

Dead-Heading Roses

(Tralee Town Park)

Everything greener, heavier, darker with rain,
releasing strong but subtle smells
like eucalyptus leaves between your hands.

You could feel the silence of students
just inside the convent wall;
exam time coming to an end.

A day you need to get inside the gardener's head,
find the mechanism that lets him spend all day
dead-heading roses.

Instead you head for the shops,
splash out, stuff your face,
anything to stay on the wagon.

Romeo And Juliet
for Coleman

Whisked off to the cinema
in the middle of the afternoon
in the first full flush of middle age.
You a Montague, me a Capulet,
a New Age Romeo and Juliet.

You would have made a better Romeo
with your Karma and kind eyes.
You would have stepped your fingers
slowly down her spinal cord
and massaged her stiff neck.
You would have held her head
in your hands for hours,
her body liquifying in your arms
and she would have entered heaven
without poison, guns or swords.

Between straining to hear Shakespearean lines
and trying to take Hell's Angels seriously,
I knew that an older woman and a younger man
would have made it more believable
in an age where the new Romeo has no problem
leaving Juliet to walk home in the pouring rain.

The Puppet Fiddler

for Martin Hayes

I would like to pull your strings
between two large stone statues
down the Champs-Elysées.
We would draw mighty crowds.

Your soft umber curls would fly
back and forth in two-time,
your body would rock and your feet
only barely touch the ground,
your arm would have a string all to itself,
your bow having free rein
and plenty of resin.

I would explain to the Parisians
that your music has no name, no story,
that even its tradition is questionable,
knowing that they wouldn't understand
this soft Celtic Clare understating.

If I met you on the street tomorrow
I might not recognise you, you
could be just as rigid as the rest of us.

Eclipse

A fat honeybee sprawls in front of the open door,
cats toss live mice until they scream to be dead,
orange tipped butterflies wish to be caterpillars,
bird soloists drowned by a soulful strimmer,
nettles and ivy choking a sour apple tree.

One can step over mill wheels, cartwheels, concrete blocks,
slabs of stone, shards of slate, trunks of trees, pots of pink petunia,
busy lizzie, three-year-old geraniums, trailing nasturtiums,
and the bee we thought was dead now hangs onto lobelia.

We settle for minor traumas here, manageable chaos,
newspapers and books littering the sitting room floor,
moisturizers, sunscreen, lipsticks clutter the dressing table,
the telephone directory in the wrong place.

There's a hole in the kitchen floor,
a smell of silage from our neighbour's yard,
plastic still covers the patio door;

and I'm supposed to get excited about Wednesday.

Eoin

He wore a hole in the carpet
dancing off his frustrations,

his father wears a frown
worrying about a hole in the carpet.

Kentucky To The Skellig Rock

Some days I feel like going home,
I miss the cat, the sea, the food.
Here they can only fry chicken one way.

At times like these I think of how I climbed
seven hundred vertical stone steps,
saw how each was spliced together,
how not one of them shook under my weight,
how celibate men channelled their energy,
their chapel, their beehive huts, their graves.

The sea I didn't have to look at until I reached the top
is like the tomorrow I don't have to think about today.
I know I can climb anything if I focus only on one step
and homesickness need only ever be for one day.

Mature Student At The Virgin Megastore

The cherry blossom spreads herself
like a whore on her wedding night,
bouquets of blue aubrietia
cling to gaps in stone walls.
The pavements are full of dog shit
but I walk everywhere.

I browse the bookshops,
have my hair cut when
my grant comes through,
buy the Irish Times and The Examiner for 50p,
pride myself that I haven't been mugged yet.

I take Nietzshe and Kierkegaard to bed
with a couple of ring doughnuts from Spierans,
discuss Plath in the canteen and
despair of ever writing a *mammy* poem.
I have analysed Joyce and *The Dead* to death
and Seamus Heaney leaves me as cold as the thought
of Ireland and England cavorting between the sheets.

I have learnt the Theory of Communication
but prefer to talk to people without
having to consult Shannon and Weaver.
But it's great fun watching the academics,
wondering what they're like as lovers –
if they insist on using the big words.

* *Mary Immaculate College, Limerick, affectionately known as
The Virgin Megastore*

My Son's Banana Suit

On the subway
between Sunnyside in Queens
and the French restaurant
in Times Square
you told me
how much
you hated it,
that you called it
your *banana suit*.

Your forced laugh
echoed through tunnels
under the Hudson river
into the homes of people
who never saw you
in that canary-yellow suit.

Just before Grand Central,
I saw your eyes framed
with my father's dark brows,
your forehead furrowed and deep
as you told me how you felt
the day your father and your brother left,
how, for the past ten years you'd blamed me.
As far as you were concerned I might as well have died.

I got it wrong, like the *banana suit*,
foolishly thinking that in not telling you the truth
I was protecting you.

The Space Between Recognition

for Ronan

In the time it takes to discover
that the face you saw
is not the face you think you saw
the waters break

and I am standing beneath your skyscraper
while you tack wooden shuttering to its roof
adding yet another layer of concrete to New York.
I, who only ever reached the height of steeples,
see a boy with steel nails held between his teeth,
a carpenter's pouch slung from his narrow hips
hammering out that dead slow beat,
Sorree, Sorree, is all that you can say...

The boy with the Sanskrit skin
comes face to face with the Chrysler Building,
the Empire State Building, Trump Tower.
A far cry from the sunbleached summers in Castlegregory,
being eaten alive by midges in Glenteenasig Wood.
With all that mass concrete between us
I'm just left with the daylight stolen from you in hugs.

The Discovery Of America

for Jackie

The Spanish guide points to St. Helen
with the symbolic gold band around her head,
This is Gala, she says, *Dali's beloved Gala,*
stolen from the poet Eluard,
but we could forgive him anything.
All is fair in love and art.

She explains how the model for Columbus
did not want to be recognised
so Dali elongates his face
and curls his hair before he
steps onto American soil.
The other three versions he profiles.
How famous this man would become
for wanting to remain unknown.

Outside in the January sun,
we took photographs on seats with melting clocks.

The Hallucinogenic Toreador

The only difference between me and a madman
*is that I am not mad – **Salvador Dali.***

Driving alongside Tampa Bay there is no warning
that St. Petersburg is home to the Hallucinogenic Toreador.
Conceived in an art supply store,
he emerges from the shadows of Venus de Milo;
her green skirt becomes his necktie,
her stomach his chin,
her waist his mouth
and her left breast his nose.
The red skirt on the second Venus becomes his cape,
the tear in his eye is shed for the fate of the bull
and a gadfly becomes the bull's eye.

The dying bull emerges from Cape Creus
where the flies of Narcisco failed to prevent the invasion of tourists.

At the top left hand corner Gala scowls in disgust.

In the bottom right hand corner, Dali –
a small boy in a sailor's suit,
holding a hoop and fossil bone,
gadflies heading towards him and his mismatched shadow.

No wonder Dali said, *This is all of Dali in one painting.*

The Flymaker

Sitting on a high stool
in a cluttered comfortable space
she strips feathers furiously to create wings.

Bodies are silk thread deftly wound,
exotic orange tails stand on their backs,
and she never has to unwind.

He displays them in glass cases –
and to the fishermen who queue at the door
she only charges seventy-five pence.

Hopefully, she will pass on her craft
because as every woman knows
the rivers are full of foolish fish.

Have You Ever Tried Burning A Piano?

Every morning
I shovel the ebony ash
to a spot in the garden
where a thrush sings.

In removing
the chill from my toes
I have strangled the inner screams
of a scale and silenced concertos.

The Geography Of Objects

I set the table,
lit the candles,
fixed the lamp
backwards an inch,
forwards a fraction,
threw a burnt sienna shawl casually
over the second-hand Lloyd Loom,
asking *him* not to laugh at my perfectionism.

She didn't say it in so many words, but
implied that she couldn't bring her friends,
no car could survive those potholes.
She wouldn't eat a meal,
wasn't long after eating,
wouldn't stay the night,
preferring the comfort of her own bed.

Then she proceeded to tell me about Joan
who was building a big house on two acres of land,
but of course she works very hard.
You'd hardly see what you've done here, she said,
ignoring my herb garden, my late summer flower bed.

She hugged me when she left.
She never used to do that.

Paul Durcan's Idea Of Heaven

He's got a headache,
he's had it all day.
He watches football on television.
I read the Sunday newspapers.
An interview with Paul Durcan
says that Paul's idea of heaven
is finding a compatible woman to live with.
Back to my man again –
Birmingham didn't win, they drew.
He consults a cookery book,
bakes a batch of teacakes,
makes me tea,
takes a nap.

He's still got the headache.
I prepare a pot of Irish stew,
we both watch Coronation Street.
After dinner the phone rings,
it's one of his women friends
he says, *yes, yes it's fine,*
everything is great,
becomes animated,
discusses our trip to Amsterdam –
two for the price of one
with the Quinnsworth tokens.
He told her I was back in Limerick,
how we slept in my room
on Friday night in a single bed.
There was a pause at that – then a laugh.

He tells her about his job,
how he loves the kids
and all that technology,
talks about our new home
and how it's coming along.
Then he tells her he's got to finish the ironing.
He neglected to tell her about the teacakes.
Needless to say, he slept on the couch last night.

Where I Came From

When you told me you loved me
but couldn't live with me,
that I might as well be drinking –
an electrical current travelled
up the backs of my legs
stopping short of my heart,
lodging itself between muscle and bone.
I forget easily where I came from,
it took you to remind me.
That winter the garden was never emptier,
my robins went elsewhere.
It was Spring before I discovered
there was another woman.

Relics

The night you left
I slept between used sheets
savouring your smell for the last time.

In the morning
I turned back the covers,
picked each abandoned hair
examining them forensically
making sure they were all yours.

You told me you brought her to our home
vehemently denying fucking her in our bed.
I didn't believe you.

I keep thinking of you in bed with her
showing her the ropes,
(the ropes that took six years to perfect)
while placing each wiry greying relic
into my dead mother's pill box.

My Mother's Diary

in memory of Kit

I found a small red diary in your drawer –

Changed the sheets today, cleaned the sitting room,
Ann and Frank called, had a bath, Teresa phoned,
went to the grave, paid ESB, pains bad.

I was writing in my journal when the phone rang the morning you died –

Dear God, I haven't written for a few days because I was in a bad
state. I think I may have been angry with you God, for taking away the
man I love. I threatened to take some tablets at the weekend, if the
pain got bad enough, but I didn't have the courage. I think I may have
*frightened my friends though... (*18th March 2002*).*

I left for the hospital not knowing that you were already dead.

We had the same doctor, he told me once
that the difference between us
was that *I* knew I was fucked up, you didn't.

I'm driving around in your car, I haven't washed it in weeks.
You had four thousand miles on the clock in three years,
I have eighteen thousand in nine months.
I wear the wedding ring that never came off your finger
until the pains got so bad they had to force it off.
I use your umbrella every day.

I wish all the things you gave out about
had been written into your diary,
but then, a diary the size of a prayer book
couldn't contain all that anger...

I don't have to spend a week
psyching myself up to phone you any more
or take deep breaths, counting to ten
before arriving at your door.
Now I say *thank you Kit* when I'm driving through
Bearna, Spiddal, Lettermore, Lettermullen.
Fucked up or not I'm doing fine.

The Black Sea

Here we were talking about money on the beachfront facing the Black
Sea, phone bills, ESB bills, using two bales of briquettes a week and it
summer. We talk of winters in Spain and how a half-moon was better
than no moon. You tell me I am obsessed with my mother and my
weight, that I need to detach, take action, cut back, eat and enjoy, or
shut up. You are *so* wise. You tell me you are much healthier, never
worry about what you eat and have no time for alternative therapies.
I've just had ten days of mud baths, hydrotherapy, electrotherapy,
massage, and a herbal concoction that has given me either diarrhoea or
detoxification. We end the night with lemon pancakes and ice cream not
knowing that it was to be our last holiday together. Your life didn't work
out the way you planned and last winter you sent me a suicide note just
when I was getting my life back. When I see you now, you look awful. I
lost all that weight when you left and my mother managed to die last year.

Moving House

I have great difficulty parting with things,
have to go through everything meticulously
before throwing them into the skip.

Sea grass baskets of photographs for safe keeping –
Paris, Amsterdam, New York, Christmas in Tunisia.
There's not one that captures your rage when you ask,
Why do you have to bring home a birdcage?
You are smiling in all of them.

The leaves began to free fall from the trees today,
the wind came from nowhere without warning.
I searched between your eyes and the fullness of your mouth
for disillusionment, but photographs are all lies.

Three times I've thrown out that framed first poem
in which you tell me that time spent without me
is like mud clinging to your boots,
that time spent with me is like sand between your fingers.
I have now thrown it where you are sure to find it.

We played house like I did when I was a child,
up the garden path, each room marked out with stones.
I read somewhere that when you move house
it takes three days for your soul to catch up.
Three days is nothing.

Grey Areas

Travelling up in the confined space of the metallic lift
we stood facing one another.

Imagine! It would have been inappropriate to kiss you
despite the fact that you had tongued my most intimate parts.

You showed me the bare balconies
and the great view of the railway station.

You showed me the bedroom, the bed still unmade
my eyes searching for KY jelly or a carelessly dropped panty.

You made me tea and I had bread and jam
though I rarely eat jam, my eyes drawn to a picture

of Irish construction workers eating their lunch
balancing on a beam high up over NYC in the thirties.

Over the fireplace the Mona Lisa was sectioned into squares.
On my way out, there was no escaping the metallic grey of the lift.

The Woman Who Looks Like A Woman Who Makes Jam

The waitress in the Grand Hotel
thought she looked like a woman who makes jam.

When I saw her picture
I agreed, and bitch that I am
told him that I thought
she looked quite ordinary,
to which he replied –
without I might add
the safety of the long pause –
I think she's stunning.

For a fraction of a nanosecond I wished
I looked like a woman who makes jam

Finding Myself In Stone

These are my rocks, there is no doubt
they have been waiting for me
whispering my name for decades –
deep veined cracks muffled by moss,
lichen and wind defiant heather.

I thought I'd find myself –
in fields of buttercups and Friesian cows,
in the cherry tree at the bottom of Jer Mack's,
the creamery cheque every month,
the kids, our own spuds.

I thought I'd found myself –
in the old Mill House with the clematis
immortalised in a poem about growing old,
the bluebelled wood, the river bank,
I was sure this was it; but no –

I had to be satisfied with stone,
few trees, a scarcity of birds
and gale force Atlantic winds.
Now and then I hear the incoherent
mumbling of monks and feel at home.

Hoovering In Lettermullen

It's almost six o'clock and I've nothing done.
I keep putting off the hoovering.
The sheets need changing for my aunt
who's visiting from London next week.
The chairs still piled with clothes
that need sorting and it's almost summer.
I open all the windows – it's that kind of day –
heat the remains of last night's Korma,
eat two crunchy Braeburn apples
phone my granddaughter to wish her a happy birthday –
the call is short – she has to get back to her bouncing castle.

I listen to Jacques Brel and Nina Simone,
smile at a Raymond Carver poem where he says,
...and sex, what is sex if it is not unbridled?
He dedicates it to his wife.

Went for a walk as far as the spot where I can sit
and smell the seaweed trapped between two islands.
And I still have nothing done but I've had a lovely day dodging it,
having little breaks between doing nothing and thinking about it,
wondering what he'll bring from the new Dundrum shopping centre,
if it will be practical like the shelving or the gadget for unscrewing jars.
Simone is winding down and the sun has moved right round the house.
It's time to climb the stairs and bring down that Hoover.

The Arrival Of The Cuckoo

You announce the arrival of the cuckoo
as if it were an everyday occurrence,
as if you didn't know I had been waiting
for that perfect iamb trapped in the throat
of a transitory bird all the way from Africa.

– Remember the poet on the podium on Saturday
the one convinced that the butterfly landing
on her sleeve was her mother –

But how could you know,
you weren't here last year when the cuckoo came –
when that persistent sound could be heard
from Lettermore to Lettermullen –
settling on the telegraph pole in my garden
right on the edge of Garumna Island –

or that for the first time since you'd left
I realised I was not alone.

Garumna Island

in memory of Michael Rua

It's February and burning bushes
merge with bruise and orange skies.
Abandoned cars line a narrow ledge,
worn out fridges, plastic cans
skirt the water's edge.

Splinters of light circling Inis Mór,
the swelling of Spring tides,
the occasional bark of a dog –
nights folding away naturally.

By day, daffodils and yellow gorse
break the monotony of dry-stone walls.
A surrogate husband provides me
with pullets' eggs and mackerel straight from the sea.
I bring him cigarettes duty-free.

Cattle short of grass patrol the roads
tied from neck to thigh. Quick to discover gaps
they join the Buddha, Chinese flute player,
feed on *my* expensive plants.

The Anointing

While seagulls swoop for scraps
I whip my knickers off
across from the Galway Bay Hotel
in the middle of the noon day.

Walkers stride the Prom oblivious to the
overbearing innuendo of RTE's Joe Duffy
or the glare of a taxi driver
who thinks I have parked in his space.
The mobile rings and I jump.

In a Richard Gere sort of voice
he tells me he is lost,
that he couldn't find the Dock Road
but that he is now passing
a place called Angels
and I am to look out for
his electric blue Yaris.

We are in Bishop Casey territory
taking well over an hour to get to my place
where we begin as if on a mission or crusade
to solemnly anoint each room,
christen each and every crevice,
cry out in every holy place.

The dust mites thinking
it's Easter Sunday
begin to sing
The Hallelujah Chorus
(as Gaeilge).

I had waited a year and a half for this
despite having been told
by my mother years ago
that I'd catch cold if I so much
as *sat* on a limestone step
without my knickers.

* Angels: a Lap Dancing Club
* As Gaeilge: In Irish

Issues

We chatted for hours over tea in Jury's where he explained
the ISEQ, FTSE, NASDAQ and DOW,
for this I will be eternally grateful.
He even held my hand, brushed my cheek leaving.

Last week I asked him to be honest,
to let me know if this was going anywhere.
He said he had some issues:
first, there was the question of height –
he was six foot one, I was four foot eleven in my socks.
Then there was the question of weight
but we won't go into that.
Then comes the real problem,
the fact that I didn't have a *sustainable* income.

Everything in his life fitted into a little box – except me.
Another one not only bites the dust but hopefully chokes on it.

Reality Lovers

for Neil

Together we watch the sun disappear
from our deeper, watery horizon,
and it was all about just being there –
while on the other side, apart from birds
there is the awful sound of alarm clocks,
millions of eyelids closing for those extra forty seconds,
women being gently fucked, lights turned on,
baths drawn, showers taken, breakfasts rushed,
coffees grabbed, early morning news, trains to catch.

Some will stop to watch the sun come up,
perhaps one or two will imagine it going down
leaving just a blood soaked sky, water to cross
and two lovers turning, heading for home.

For My Fifty-Fifth Birthday

For my fifty-fifth birthday
I *don't* want another leather bag,
or a comfortable pair of Ecco shoes,
or a hand-painted headscarf,
or a voucher for a Golden Years' weekend,
or even an hour's facial in the Radisson
or a year's subscription to Oprah.

What I *do* want for my fifty-fifth birthday
is a purple butterfly tattooed
between my navel and vagina
so that when the doctor visits
the nursing home in my ninety-fifth year
and everything else is shrivelled,
every faculty faulty or missing,
he will know forty years ago there was this woman
with a skittish sense of fun who found love
at fifty-five and marked it with a purple butterfly.

Marion Moynihan, originally from Kanturk, in North Cork, began writing seriously while living in Kerry in the 1990's. She studied English Literature and Theology at Mary Immaculate College in Limerick, and Psychology and Creative Writing in Thomas Moore College, Kentucky, where she received an award for editing the college magazine, *Words*. In 2002 she completed an MA in Writing at NUIG as well as renovating a cottage in Connemara, where she now holds weekend writing courses. In 2005 she was the winner of County Galway's *Firewords Award* and awarded the *Publication Assistance Award 2006* from Galway County Council. *The Moon's Daughter* is her first collection of poems.

Also available from DOGHOUSE:

Heart of Kerry -- an anthology of writing
from performers at Poet's Corner, Harty's Bar, Tralee 1992-2003

Song of the Midnight Fox - Eileen Sheehan

Loose Head & Other Stories - Tommy Frank O'Connor

Both Sides Now - Peter Keane

Shadows Bloom / Scáthanna Faoi Bhláth - haiku by John W. Sexton,
translations into Irish by Gabriel Rosenstock

FINGERPRINTS (On Canvas) - Karen O'Connor

Vortex - John W. Sexton

Apples In Winter - Liam Aungier

The Waiting Room - Margaret Galvin

I Met A Man... Gabriel Rosenstock

The DOGHOUSE book of **Ballad Poems**

Every DOGHOUSE book costs €12, postage free, to anywhere in the
world (& other known planets). Cheques, Postal Orders (or any legal
method) payable to DOGHOUSE,
also PAYPAL (www.paypal.com) to doghousepaypal@eircom.net

*"Buy a full set of DOGHOUSE books, in time they will be
collectors' items"* **- Gabriel Fitzmaurice, April 12, 2005.**

DOGHOUSE
P.O. Box 312
Tralee G.P.O.
Tralee
Co. Kerry
Ireland
tel + 353 6671 37547
email doghouse312@eircom.net   www.doghousebooks.ie